MW01168946

Ten To One Rum
Presents

Kindred
Spirits

A Celebration of Black
Excellence in Craft Cocktails

Black History Month
2022 Special Edition

Ten To One Rum Presents

Kindred Spirits: A Celebration of
Black Excellence in Craft Cocktails

www.tentoonerum.com

First Edition
Copyright © 2022 Ten To One Rum
ISBN: 978-0-578-34799-8

Illustrations by Erick M. Ramos

Designed in the U.S.
Printed by Bedwick & Jones, PA, U.S.

For Sandra Welch-Farrell and Terrence Farrell,
and in Memory of Diana Welch and Una Farrell,
who taught me the virtue of standing on the
shoulders of those who've come before you.

Forward, together as one.

Contents

Foreword

Acknowledgments

Cocktails

Specialty Ingredients

Foreword

by Marc-Kwesi Farrell

From the earliest days of Ten To One's inception, we have set out on a mission to continuously challenge expectations, and change the way that people taste, experience and talk about rum. In our view, this has been as much a journey to introduce consumers to a more contemporary and inspired view of the spirit, as it has been providing an authentic window into the broader culture and heritage that surrounds it.

In celebration of Black History Month, we stand proudly on the shoulders of those who have come before us. It is not commonly known that bartenders like Tom Bullock, the first Black man to have a cocktail manual published, were some of the earliest pioneers of the craft cocktail art form. Many of those innovations have been overlooked across the broader industry, a pattern too often repeated even today. This book honors their legacy and celebrates the many creators making waves across the world of craft cocktails today.

In this, our first edition of Kindred Spirits, we highlight 28 talented Black bartenders from around the country, who have developed 28 incredible cocktail recipes - one for each day of the month of February.

Together we offer this manual as a tribute to all the amazing Black men and women whose creative contributions, imagination, and flair, paved the way for what we are able to create and share today.

These cocktails can, and should, be enjoyed all-year-round. So irrespective of where you are in your craft cocktail journey, we hope you will keep the manual close by, as an able companion in providing moments of inspiration, celebration and joy.

We are proud to welcome you to this broader collective; one that hopes to play a small role in driving our industry forward by continuing to champion and celebrate a broad spectrum of creative voices with amazing stories to tell. We have no doubt you will enjoy these outstanding cocktails and look forward to seeing you bring the magic of these exceptional bartenders to life.

Cheers!

Marc-Kwesi Farrell
Founder & CEO
Ten To One Rum

Acknowledgments

A special thank you to all those who
made Kindred Spirits possible.

Our 28 outstanding bartenders:
    Andra Johnson
    Anthony Baker
    Anthony Bates
    Beau Bradley
    Brittany Triche
    Camille Wilson
    Chauncey Smith
    Derek Jeffries
    Erin Birmingham
    Ezana Million
    Franky Marshall
    French Marshall
    Karl Williams
    Kern Rodriguez
    Keyatta Mincey Parker
    Kia Palmer
    Marcio Ramos
    Maya Taylor
    Ramón Clark
    Ramona Jackson
    Raquel Ravenell & Erika Moore
    Rori Robinson
    Shane Smith
    Shannon Mustipher
    Shelarys Nolasco
    Tiffanie Barriere
    Tokiwa Sears
    Treaser Brumskine

Illustration:
    Erick Ramos

Design:
    Oscar Pipson

Production:
    Caroline Snizek

Kindred Spirits

28 Inspired Bartenders and Cocktail Recipes

The "Piña Colada" Old-Fashioned

by Anthony "the Professor" Baker

Inspiration

As someone who teaches online cocktail classes, I get to meet a lot of people, many of whom have different taste preferences. Classes are usually split by those that prefer a more balanced drink and those that prefer something a little more spirit-forward.

During my rum themed class, the Piña Colada is a big hit. I came to notice that while it's not considered a strong drink, everyone enjoys the pineapple and coconut flavor combination. Wanting to incorporate these flavors into a more spirit-forward drink I developed the 'Piña Colada' Old Fashioned, a cocktail that allows the rum to shine amongst delightful hints of pineapple and coconut.

Taste

Light	Spirit Forward

Dry	Sweet

Skill & Prep

Easy	Advanced

Minutes	Hours

Ingredients

2 ½ oz	Ten To One Dark Rum
¼ oz	Monin Pineapple Syrup
½ oz	Kalani Coconut Rum Liqueur
3-4 ds	Angostura Bitters
gn	Pineapple Leaf
	Dried Pineapple Wedge

Instructions

01.	Add all ingredients to your glass.
02.	Add a large ice cube.
03.	Stir for 10 seconds until cold.
04.	Garnish and serve.

Glassware

Rocks

Frenchman's Cove

by French "Scotty" Marshall

Inspiration

This cocktail was inspired by one of my favorite places; a beautiful hidden oasis in Portland, Jamaica known as Frenchman's Cove. Secluded with soft golden sands and sapphire water, the serenity of this beach is unmatched.

The Frenchman's Cove cocktail was designed to be enjoyed during the transition from day to night, as the sun sets on the cove. The slight funk from the passion fruit and effervescence from sparkling wine allows you to close out the day at the beach and welcome an evening full of festivities to come.

Taste

Light ———— Spirit Forward

Dry ———— Sweet

Skill & Prep

Easy ———— Advanced

Minutes ———— Hours

Ingredients

1 oz	Ten To One White Rum
¼ oz	Passion Fruit Purée*
¼ oz	Lemon Juice
½ oz	Martini Fiero
¾ oz	Simple Syrup*
	Sparkling Wine
gn	Orange Peel

Instructions

01. Add all ingredients (excl. sparkling wine) to a shaker tin with ice & shake for 10 seconds.
02. Double strain into your glass.
03. Top with sparkling wine.
04. Garnish and serve.

Glassware

Nick & Nora

Crown Swizzle

by Shannon Mustipher

Inspiration

Named after the Trinidadian hotel where it was first concocted in the 1920s the Queens Park Swizzle is a highly underrated cocktail and one of my all-time favorite rum drinks. Often mistaken for a Mojito, the Swizzle is a far more complex cocktail experience that utilizes dark rum and bitters.

The Crown Swizzle is my take on this classic, which uses a combination of Ten To One Dark and White rum to create a delicious drinking experience that highlights a combination of the best rum characteristics found throughout the Caribbean. This simple construction with classic roots will elicit your curiosity & have you wanting to learn more about Ten To One and the origins of rum found in its delicious blend.

Taste

Light ———————————— Spirit Forward

Dry ———————————— Sweet

Skill & Prep

Easy ———————————— Advanced

Minutes ———————————— Hours

Ingredients

1 ½ oz	Ten To One Dark Rum
½ oz	Ten To One White Rum
¼ oz	Allspice Dram
½ oz	Key Lime Juice
½ oz	Demerara Syrup
5-6	Mint Sprigs
3 ds	Angostura Bitters
gn	Mint Sprigs
	Orange Peel

Glassware

Collins

Instructions

01. In your glass muddle the mint leaves and lime juice.
02. Add Ten To One White Rum and fill glass with Ice. Stir to chill.
03. Add Ten To One Dark Rum.
04. Top with allspice dram & Angostura Bitters, adding additional ice if needed.
05. Garnish and serve.

Breakfast In Paradise

by Keyatta Mincey Parker

Inspiration

Born and raised in Paynesville, Liberia, I hold rum very close to my heart. Not only is it a staple in many local bars and liquor cabinets, but it also runs in my family. I grew up learning about rum from my uncle, Uncle Toussaint who for many years has distilled his own rum.

Breakfast in Paradise honors my family legacy while celebrating many of my favorite local ingredients that are culturally significant to the Paynesville region. Whether buying fresh pineapples at the street markets or taking turmeric to help with recovery and healing, all ingredients come together in a bright and vibrant cocktail that embodies both me and my story.

Taste

Light	Spirit Forward

Dry	Sweet

Skill & Prep

Easy	Advanced

Minutes	Hours

Ingredients

1 ½ oz	Ten To One White Rum
½ oz	Ten To One Dark Rum
1 oz	Pineapple Turmeric Syrup*
1 oz	Aquafaba
½ oz	Lemon Juice
¼ oz	Pineapple Juice
gn	Cracked Black Pepper

Instructions

01. Add all ingredients to a shaker tin with ice and shake vigorously for 10 seconds.
02. Strain into your glass.
03. Garnish and serve.

Glassware

Coupe

The
Last One

by Marcio Ramos

Inspiration

The Last One is constructed to take you on a journey to the Caribbean, transporting you to a warm beach with a cool breeze blowing in your hair.

Like many bartenders, my two favorite spirits are rum and chartreuse, so it was a no brainer for me to combine them in this special cocktail recipe. Chartreuse can be a tricky spirit to work with, often overpowering any other spirit used in combination. To create a well-balanced drink that allows the rum to shine, I developed a chartreuse based foam to top the cocktail that compliments the rum and adds a sweet frothy taste upfront.

Taste

Light	Spirit Forward

Dry	Sweet

Skill & Prep

Easy	Advanced

Minutes	Hours

Ingredients

2 oz	Ten To One Dark Rum
¾ oz	Wild Strawberry Syrup*
½ oz	Saint Germain
½ oz	Lime Juice
½ oz	Lemon Juice
	Green Chartreuse Foam*
gn	Berry or Lime Zest

Instructions

01. Add all ingredients (excl. green chartreuse foam) to a shaker tin with ice and shake vigorously for 10 seconds.
02. Double strain into your glass.
03. Top with green chartreuse foam.
04. Garnish and serve.

Glassware

Rocks

Monks Mood

by Shane Smith

Inspiration

Monks Mood is inspired by one of the most iconic and innovative jazz musicians of our time, Thelonious Monk. Monk fashioned a startlingly unique, inimitable playing and composing style that influenced virtually every succeeding jazz generation. He was a master of the musical alphabet.

This cocktail encapsulates the swing, groove and tempo he made famous in his music and speaks to the beautiful and harmonious blend of Caribbean rums found in Ten To One.

Taste

Light	Spirit Forward
Dry	Sweet

Skill

Easy	Advanced
Minutes	Hours

Ingredients

1 ½ oz	Ten To One Dark Rum
¾ oz	Lemon Juice
¾ oz	Orgeat*
1 ds	Angostura Bitters
2 ds	Eucalyptus Bitters
gn	Spiked Lemon Peel Eucalyptus Stem

Instructions

01. Add all ingredients to a shaker tin with ice and shake vigorously for 10 seconds.
02. Double strain into your glass.
03. Garnish and serve.

Glassware

Nick & Nora

2 Birds, 1 Stone

by Tokiwa Sears

Inspiration

I constructed 2 Birds, 1 Stone to offer a healthy moment of reprieve from the stresses of everyday life. I call it self care in a glass, If you're searching for a refreshing and balanced cocktail to put you at ease, look no further.

A delightful mix of ginger, turmeric, and fresh fruit that pairs wonderfully with Ten To One Dark Rum, this cocktail will put a smile on your face and have you feeling relaxed and ready to take on the world anew.

Taste

Light	Spirit Forward

Dry	Sweet

Skill & Prep

Easy	Advanced

Minutes	Hours

Ingredients

2 oz	Ten To One Dark Rum
¾ oz	Lime Juice
¾ oz	Ginger Turmeric Syrup*
3 ds	Bookers Bitters
1	Strawberry
gn	Strawberry Fruit Leather
	Edible Gold Dust

Instructions

01. Muddle Strawberry in the bottom of a shaker tin.
02. Add remaining ingredients to the shaker tin with ice & shake vigorously for 10 seconds.
03. Strain into your glass.
04. Garnish and serve.

Glassware

Coupe

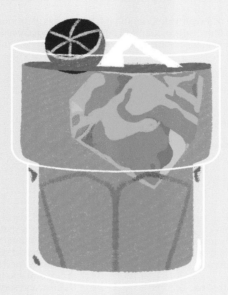

The Tenicillin

by Ezana Million

Inspiration

There's nothing like a little rum to provide a good pick me up during the Fall season. The Tenicillin is a Ten To One twist on the classic Penicillin, a cocktail widely regarded as a cure-all that has been used to keep spirits high and sinuses clear since its inception in the early 2000s.

A sweet, tart, spicy and delicious cocktail, The Tenicillin is an easy drinking take on a cult classic with just enough booze and ginger to keep all those winter blues at bay.

Taste

Light	Spirit Forward

Dry	Sweet

Skill & Prep

Easy	Advanced

Minutes	Hours

Ingredients

1 ½ oz	Ten To One Dark Rum
½ oz	Ten To One White Rum
1 oz	Pineapple Juice
¾ oz	Lemon Juice
1 tsp	Fresh Ginger; grated
½ oz	Honey Syrup*
gn	Dehydrated Lemon

Instructions

01. Add all ingredients to a shaker tin with ice and shake vigorously for 10 seconds.
02. Fine strain into your glass over ice.
03. Garnish and serve.

Glassware

Rocks

Les Plantes

by Rori Robinson

Inspiration

Inspired to reimagine a traditional tropical cocktail, the Les Plantes is a smooth sipping drink that looks to highlight the clear expression of fresh plants found in Ten To One Rum; from the aromatic flowers and green grass to the tropical fruits and spices.

A balanced cocktail that adds complementary fruits and herbs, Les Plantes avoids the overly cloying sugar taste that has become the stereotype of mixed rum and tiki-style drinks. No one ingredient dominates in this cocktail, as all flavors are experienced equally both on the nose and palate.

Taste

Light ———————————— Spirit Forward

Dry ———————————— Sweet

Skill & Prep

Easy ———————————— Advanced

Minutes ———————————— Hours

Ingredients

1 ½ oz	Ten To One White Rum
½ oz	Ten To One Dark Rum
½ oz	Bloom Bar Garnish Company Pineapple Ginger Syrup
½ oz	Coconut Creme*
2 ds	Orange Bitters
gn	Sprig of Basil

Instructions

01. Add all ingredients to a shaker tin with ice and shake vigorously for 10 seconds.
02. Double strain into a chilled glass.
03. Garnish and serve.

Glassware

Nick & Nora

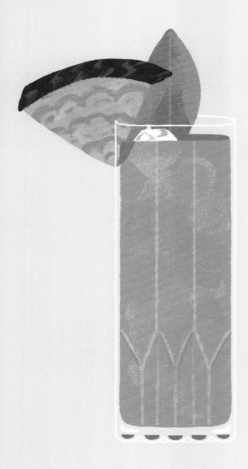

Bitter Sweet Punch

by Camille Wilson

Inspiration

The Bitter Sweet Punch is my take on a classic rum punch and an ode to my Caribbean heritage. In Caribbean Culture, rum punch is a big deal, no celebration is complete without it, and no one recipe is the same with every maker putting their unique spin on things.

Most traditional rum punch recipes have a base of lime juice, pineapple juice, and sweetener, and mine is no different. To add my personal touch, however, I've incorporated Amaro Lucano to give it a slightly bitter and herbal taste that creates a surprising twist and unexpected but delightful extra layer of flavor.

Taste

Light	Spirit Forward
Dry	Sweet

Skill & Prep

Easy	Advanced
Minutes	Hours

Ingredients

1 ½ oz	Ten To One Dark Rum
¾ oz	Amaro Lucano
½ oz	Lime Juice
¾ oz	Cinnamon Syrup*
1 oz	Pineapple Juice
gn	Pineapple Leaf
	Dried Pineapple Wedge

Instructions

01. Add all ingredients to a shaker tin with ice and shake vigorously for 10 seconds.
02. Pour into your glass over ice.
03. Garnish and serve.

Glassware

Collins

The Fantum

by Ms. Franky Marshall

Inspiration

Growing up in a household full of rum drinkers it was naturally the first spirit I ever experimented with and subsequently holds a special place in my heart. It wasn't until I started crafting cocktails however that I took a serious interest in the spirit, learning about all the different styles and flavor profiles that make rum so versatile and compelling.

The Fantum, named after its ghostly appearance is a playful cocktail that incorporates one of my favorite flavor combinations: Green Tea and Coconut. When mixed with the baked apple and spices found in Ten To One Dark Rum along with the orange and vanilla from Parfait Amour you get a bright drink with a rich combination of aromas for you to explore.

Taste

Light	Spirit Forward
Dry	Sweet

Skill & Prep

Easy	Advanced
Minutes	Hours

Ingredients

1 ½ oz	Green Tea Infused Ten To One Dark Rum*
½ oz	Parfait Amour Liqueur
½ oz	Coconut Milk
¼ oz	Cane Sugar Syrup*
gn	Grated Coconut Orange Zest

Glassware

Stemmed

Instructions

01. Add all ingredients to a shaker tin with ice and shake vigorously for 10 seconds.
02. Pour into your glass.
03. Garnish and serve.

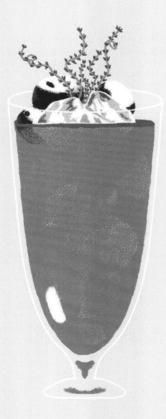

The
Big Easy

by Anthony Bates

Inspiration

There is no city quite like New Orleans. A place where African American culture has played an intrinsic role in the economic, social, and cultural development of the city. Known for its amazing cuisine and craft cocktail scene (among many other things), NOLA set a foundation for black excellence and paved the way for black people in the world of hospitality.

Inspired by my favorite city, The Big Easy pays homage to New Orleans. Utilizing a base of Ten To One Rum, this drink incorporates Burlesque Bitters and Absinthe to give it a southern twist. Fruit forward with hints of aromatic spices this cocktail will take you on a memorable journey to the south.

Taste

Light   Spirit Forward

Dry   Sweet

Skill & Prep

Easy   Advanced

Minutes   Hours

Ingredients

1 ½ oz	Ten To One White Rum
½ oz	Crème De Cassis
¼ oz	Suze Saveur d'Autrefois
¾ oz	Lemon Juice
½ oz	Honey Syrup*
2 ds	Bittermans Burlesque Bitters
	Absinthe
	Club Soda
gn	Thyme
	Frozen Grapes
	Powdered Sugar

Instructions

01. Add all ingredients (excl. absinthe & club soda) to a shaker tin with ice & shake vigorously for 10 seconds.
02. Strain into an absinthe rinsed glass over ice.
03. Top with club soda.
04. Garnish and serve.

Glassware

Hurricane

Maudell's Morning Glory

by Kia Palmer

Inspiration

Maudell's Morning Glory is inspired by my Grandmother, Maudell Ophelia Palmer who had a significant hand in raising my siblings and me, all while fostering her own children. At one point she had 10 people living in a 3 bedroom house. An incredible woman she ensured it never felt crowded, that's her power, that's her magic. What's more, we never left the house on an empty stomach. She made breakfast every day. Sometimes Cream of Wheat, sometimes grits, bacon, and eggs. Always delicious. Always made with love.

This cocktail embodies my favorite breakfast: bacon, eggs, pancakes, and orange juice. A meal my Grandmother reserved for special occasions.

Taste

Light	Spirit Forward
Dry	Sweet

Skill & Prep

Easy	Advanced
Minutes	Hours

Ingredients

2 oz	Bacon Fat Washed Ten To One Dark Rum*
1	Egg White
½ oz	Hoodoo Chicory Liqueur
½ oz	Honey Syrup*
3 ds	Angostura Bitters
gn	Black Pepper Expressed Orange Peel

Instructions

01. Add all ingredients (excl. bitters) to a shaker tin w/o ice and dry shake for 30 seconds.
02. Add ice to shaker tin and shake vigorously again.
03. Double strain into your glass.
04. Top with 3 dashes of Angostura Bitters.
05. Garnish and serve.

Glassware

Coupe

The Cortisone

by Ramón Clark

Inspiration

If you've worked in the service industry you've likely heard of a Daiquiri Time Out (DTO): a snack-size version of a daiquiri that is often used to resolve conflict, reduce tensions, or simply have a moment after a tough shift.

The Cortisone is an elevated version of a DTO inspired by the Penicillin; a citrus-forward, smoky refreshing cocktail known for its healing properties. Starting out dry and tart this cocktail has a tangy, juicy, and herbaceous finish that much like a Penicillin is sure to provide a moment of release.

Taste

Light	Spirit Forward
Dry	Sweet

Skill & Prep

Easy	Advanced
Minutes	Hours

Ingredients

1 ½ oz	Ten To One White Rum
¼ oz	Campari
¾ oz	Lime Juice
½ oz	Ginger Honey Syrup*
½ oz	Pineapple Gum Syrup*
2 ds	Angostura Bitters
gn	Grated Nutmeg

Instructions

01. Add all ingredients (excl. Campari) to a shaker tin with ice and shake vigorously for 10 to 20 seconds.
02. Double strain into your glass over a large ice cube.
03. Top with Campari.
04. Garnish and serve.

Glassware

Rocks

Split Personali-tea

by Ramona Jackson

Inspiration

The Split Personali-tea, is a savory porch sipper that transcends seasons & continents. A homage to my recent visit to South Africa I wanted to marry my African roots to my love for Korean cuisine in an East meets West cocktail.

A culinary inspired drink utilizing Ten to One White Rum and Uncle Nearest Premium Aged Whiskey, this construction blends notes of lemongrass and pepper that pair delightfully with rooibos tea (South Africa) and bulgogi syrup (Korea). A wonderful reminder to drink your dinner and travel through cocktails.

Taste

Light ———————————— Spirit Forward

Dry ———————————— Sweet

Skill & Prep

Easy ———————————— Advanced

Minutes ———————————— Hours

Ingredients

1 oz	Ten To One White Rum
1 oz	Uncle Nearest 1856 Whiskey
¾ oz	Rooibos Tea, brewed
¾ oz	Basil Mango Bulgogi Syrup*
3 ds	Angostura Bitters
1 ds	Himalayan Sea Salt
gn	Scored Mango Strip
	Basil Leaves

Instructions

01. Add all ingredients to a shaker tin with ice and shake vigorously for 10 seconds.
02. Strain into your glass.
03. Garnish and serve.

Glassware

Coupe

Adeola:
The Crown Brings Honor

by Treaser Brumskine

Inspiration

Honoring my late sister and celebrating my daughter who both share the name Adeola, this cocktail is about commemorating a legacy while teaching my daughter about her rich ancestry. I want my daughter to have an understanding and appreciation of who she is, where her family comes from, and the many beautiful cultures she is a part of.

A southern girl from Georgia who is of Liberian-Puerto Rican-Dominican Republic descent this drink incorporates ingredients that are indigenous or native to these regions. Adeola: The Crown Brings Honor is a fruit-forward cocktail that tells a rich and authentic craft cocktail story about my family and our origins.

Taste

Light ——————— Spirit Forward

Dry ——————— Sweet

Skill & Prep

Easy ——————— Advanced

Minutes ——————— Hours

Ingredients

2 oz	Plantain & Ginger Infused Ten To One White Rum*
1 oz	Mango Plum Nectar
¾ oz	Lemon Juice
½ oz	Plantain Watermelon Syrup*
gn	Watermelon, Cantaloupe, & Plantain; cubed

Instructions

01. Add all ingredients to a shaker tin with ice and shake vigorously for 10 seconds.
02. Strain into your glass over ice, watermelon, cantaloupe, & plantain cubes.

Glassware

Collins

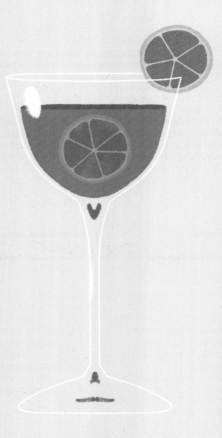

July In November

by Maya Taylor

Inspiration

A cocktail for all four seasons. Rum is often unfairly stereotyped as a summer spirit, largely due to its strong association with the Caribbean and its link to Tiki-style cocktails which often evoke an image of the beach. Rum however is an incredibly versatile spirit that is perfect for any occasion, any time of year.

July In November looks to showcase the versatility of Ten To One Rum, highlighting the grassy and herbaceous notes found in the spirit while adding a touch of sweetness and tartness through the blood orange syrup. A well-balanced cocktail that is equal parts simple and elegant.

Taste

Light	Spirit Forward
Dry	Sweet

Skill & Prep

Easy	Advanced
Minutes	Hours

Ingredients

1 ½ oz	Ten To One White Rum
½ oz	Cardamon Blood Orange Simple Syrup*
½ oz	Lime Juice
¼ oz	Blood Orange Pellegrino
gn	Dehydrated Lime Wedge

Instructions

01. Add all ingredients to a shaker tin with ice and shake vigorously for 10 seconds.
02. Strain into your glass.
03. Garnish and serve.

Glassware

Coupe

Mood 4Ever

by Brittany Triche

Inspiration

The Caribbean is home to some of my most memorable life experiences, and this cocktail is designed to mimic the sheer joy and happiness that these memories evoke. The combination of flavors reminds me of who I am and the people and places that I love.

In Mood 4Ever, the tart, but sweet flavor of the guava compliments the pineapple and island spices from the Ten To One Dark Rum. A well-balanced cocktail it will transform your mood and have you instantly craving a Pastelito.

Taste

Light ▬▬ Spirit Forward

Dry ▬▬▬▬ Sweet

Skill

Easy Advanced

Minutes ▬▬ Hours

Ingredients

1 ½ oz	Ten To One Dark Rum
½ oz	Maraschino Liqueur
½ oz	Lemon Juice
½ oz	Pineapple Juice
½ oz	Guava Juice
gn	Pineapple Leaves

Instructions

01. Add all ingredients to a shaker tin with ice and shake vigorously for 10 seconds.
02. Strain into your glass over ice.
03. Garnish and serve.

Glassware

Rocks

On Common Grounds

by Derek Jeffries

Inspiration

My love for rum is accredited to a former bar manager who challenged me to visit a local, and now world-famous rum bar to learn more about the spirit. Within a few months, my whole perspective on rum had changed. A beautifully complex spirit I was amazed at just how diverse it can be. No longer did I believe that rum had to be associated with the sweet and sugary drinks that often mask all of its character.

An approachable yet complex cocktail, On Common Grounds, is a twist on a Rum Manhattan, pairing the warm notes of banana and vanilla found in Ten To One Dark Rum with a coffee-infused Punt e Mes Vermouth which amplifies the spice notes that linger delightfully in the dark rum.

Taste

Light	Spirit Forward
Dry	Sweet

Skill & Prep

Easy	Advanced
Minutes	Hours

Ingredients

2 oz	Ten To One Dark Rum
¾ oz	Coffee-infused Punt e Mes*
2 ds	Scrappy's Aromatic Bitters
gn	Lime Peel

Glassware

Rocks

Instructions

01. Add all ingredients to a shaker tin with ice and shake vigorously for 10 seconds.
02. Strain into your glass over ice.
03. Express lime peel.
04. Garnish and serve.

Feathers to Feather

by Raquel Ravenell & Erika Moore

Inspiration

Ten To One Rum highlights some of the best rum characteristics that can be found throughout the Caribbean. From the Dominican Republic to Jamaica the blends are beautifully complex and celebrate the diversity of island culture and island life.

Feathers to Feather pays homage to this diverse yet harmonious culture utilizing flavors and textures like salt, silk, herb, smoke, and spice to honor the region and amplify the notes found in the rum.

Taste

Light	Spirit Forward
Dry	Sweet

Skill & Prep

Easy	Advanced
Minutes	Hours

Ingredients

2 oz	Ten To One Dark Rum
½ oz	Ginger Juice
1 oz	Black Cardamom Syrup*
1 oz	Oat Milk
2 pn	Pink Himalayan Salt
2	Fresh Thyme Sprigs
gn	Black Cardamon Pod
	Fresh Thyme

Instructions

01. Smack thyme between your hands to accentuate the oils from the herb and place it in the shaker tin.
02. Add all remaining ingredients to the shaker tin with ice & shake vigorously for 20 seconds.
03. Double strain into a chilled glass.
04. Garnish and serve.

Glassware

Coupe

Harlem Rose

by Shelarys Nolasco

Inspiration

Growing up in New York City, winter was always my favorite time of year, full of family gatherings, holiday celebrations and if you're lucky a little romance. Regardless of the occasion rum is always at the center of any special moment, whether it's batching a creamy Coquito, crafting an earthy Mama Juana or my personal favorite, sharing a Sorrel Punch.

Sorrel or "Rosa de Jamaica" more formally known as Hibiscus is a classic Caribbean holiday staple and is considered to bring romance and happiness. The Harlem Rose builds on this energy and liveliness and is the perfect cocktail to help you dance the night away.

Taste

Light	Spirit Forward
Dry	Sweet

Skill & Prep

Easy	Advanced
Minutes	Hours

Ingredients

2 oz	Ten To One Dark Rum
¾ oz	St. Germain
1 oz	Lime Juice
1 oz	Egg White
1 oz	Sorrel Syrup*
gn	Edible Flowers
	Hibiscus Salt*

Glassware

Coupe

Instructions

01. Wet the rim of your glass with a lime wedge and dip it in the hibiscus salt.
02. Add all ingredients to a shaker tin and dry shake w/o ice for 30 seconds.
03. Add ice to shaker tin and shake vigorously again.
04. Double strain into your glass.
05. Garnish and serve.

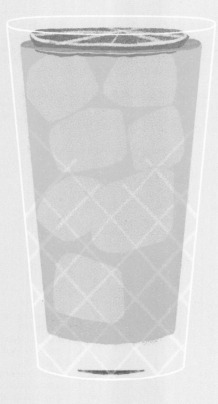

When My Two Uncles Met

by Karl Williams

Inspiration

When My Two Uncles Met is a twist on a cocktail I serve at 67 Orange Street called The Hedonist. It was inspired by a conversation with a friend who said it reminded him of a trip he had taken to Jamaica; transporting him back to the island and all the great tastes, textures and experiences he became familiar with.

Always made with a rum base, this black history month twist also incorporates two additional black-owned brands: Uncle Nearest Premium Aged Whiskey and my own ginger beer Uncle Waithley's Vincy Brew that pair beautifully with Ten To One Dark Rum.

Taste

Light	Spirit Forward
Dry	Sweet

Skill & Prep

Easy	Advanced
Minutes	Hours

Ingredients

- 1 ½ oz   Ten To One Dark Rum
- ½ oz   Uncle Nearest 1856 Whiskey
- ½ oz   Salers Aperitif
- ½ oz   Curried Simple Syrup*
- ¾ oz   Lemon Juice
- 3 ds   Creole Bitters
-    Uncle Waithley's Vincy Brew Ginger Beer

- gn   Lemon Slice

Instructions

01. Add all ingredients (excl. ginger beer) to a shaker tin with ice and shake vigorously for 10 seconds.
02. Strain into your glass over ice.
03. Top with Uncle Waithley's Vincy Brew Ginger Beer.
04. Garnish and serve.

Glassware

Collins

Black Excellence

by Beau Bradley

Inspiration

Black Excellence is a cocktail that celebrates the best of black-owned and showcases the best ingredients native to Africa in one drink. Rum is hugely popular in Caribbean and African cultures around the world, so it was naturally the spirit of choice for this cocktail.

Ten To One Dark Rum is paired with Capertif, a South African Aperitif that lightens up the cocktail, alongside Ethiopian Coffee which brings vanilla, ripe fruit and some acidity. A little Orgeat creates a sweet nutty finish that makes for a perfect evening cocktail which, honors a shared heritage and embodies black excellence.

Taste

Light	Spirit Forward
Dry	Sweet

Skill & Prep

Easy	Advanced
Minutes	Hours

Ingredients

1 ½ oz	Ten To One Dark Rum
½ oz	Caperitif
¾ oz	Ethiopian Coffee*
1 oz	Orgeat*
1 bsp	Activated Charcoal**
1 oz	Egg White
gn	Shiso Flower

Instructions

01. Add all ingredients to a shaker tin & dry shake w/o ice for 30 seconds.
02. Add ice to shaker tin and shake vigorously again.
03. Fine strain into a chilled glass.
04. Garnish and serve.

Glassware

Coupe

**Do not consume if you are taking supplements or medication.
Avoid taking within 4 hours before or after of eating food.

Rum
Scaffa

by Tiffanie Barriere

Inspiration

A Scaffa is a mixed drink stirred or layered with no ice that traditionally combines a liquor with 1-2 liqueurs. They are great for showing off the nuanced flavors and aromas of spirits like rum and whiskey. A "stacked" drink, the Scaffa utilizes slightly different densities of various liqueurs to create an array of layers that allow for a dynamic drinking experience.

A technique often reserved for the master mixologist, Scaffa cocktails were frequently found at the St Louis Country Club and Pendennis Club in Louisville, KY, where pioneering Black bartender Tom Bullock was refining his craft and serving some of the most respected and delicious cocktails in the world.

Taste

Light	Spirit Forward
Dry	Sweet

Skill

Easy	Advanced
Minutes	Hours

Ingredients

- 1 oz   Ten To One Dark Rum
- 1 oz   Maraschino Liqueur
- 1 oz   Green Chartreuse

Glassware

Port

Instructions

01. Add Green Chartreuse to a small glass.
02. Pour maraschino liqueur slowly over the backside of a bar spoon. It will drop to the bottom.
03. Top by pouring Ten To One Dark Rum slowly over the backside of a bar spoon.

Yellow No. 5

by Erin Birmingham

Inspiration

Building off the specifications of a Daiquiri, one of the most classic and elegant rum cocktails, The Yellow No.5 is an involved cocktail build with a touch of science and an elaborate garnish game.

Orange juice is used in place of lime juice with a touch of citric acid powder to boost the acidity, while a coffee-based Amaro amplifies the notes found in Ten To One Dark Rum. A spicy syrup rounds out the cocktail and adds a delightful and complex burst of flavor. Just sip, close your eyes, and dream of island life.

Taste

Light — Spirit Forward
Dry — Sweet

Skill

Easy — Advanced
Minutes — Hours

Ingredients

- ¾ oz Ten To One Dark Rum
- ¾ oz Ten To One White Rum
- ½ oz Vecchio Amaro del Capo
- ¾ oz Lemon Juice
- ¾ oz Chinese Five Spice Syrup*
- ¾ oz Acidulated OJ*

- gn Tostone
  Fennel Fronds
  Tropical Flower
  Grated Coffee Bean
  Bamboo Straw

Instructions

01. Add all ingredients to a shaker tin with ice and shake vigorously for 10 seconds.
02. Strain into your glass.
03. Top your glass with crushed ice.
04. Garnish and serve.

Glassware

Stemless Wine Glass

Spicy
Monarch

by Kern Rodriguez

Inspiration

Inspired by the unpredictability of one's journey through life and our innate ability to adapt to change, the Spicy Monarch will take you on an emotional trip through a range of flavors and textures that end up coming together in perfect harmony.

The past year has taught us a lot about ourselves. Things can change in such a short period of time; from losing loved ones to gaining new ones, from insecurity to comfort, from uncertainty to confidence and conviction. This cocktail is a celebration of that journey; all that has come before and all that's yet to come.

Taste

Light	Spirit Forward
Dry	Sweet

Skill

Easy	Advanced
Minutes	Hours

Ingredients

1 ¾ oz	Ten To One Dark Rum
¼ oz	Pernod
¾ oz	Spiced Pomegranate Cordial*
1oz	Lemon Juice
1	Lemon Peel Swath
gn	Dehydrated Chili Pepper

Instructions

01. Add all ingredients to a shaker tin with ice & shake vigorously for 10-15 seconds.
02. Strain into your glass.
03. Garnish and serve.

Glassware

Coupe

Crismus Breeze

by Andra "AJ" Johnson

Inspiration

With darkness comes clarity. Despite being raised a Jamaican-American I didn't grow up knowing a lot about my Jamaican heritage. My later father never spoke much about it. It wasn't until his father, my Papa Doey passed away that I first met any of my Jamaican relatives. Since then it's been a dream of mine to travel to Jamaica and spend 'Crismus' there.

The Crismus Breeze is a direct representation and celebration of my heritage while honoring the journey of discovery we undertake to constantly learn more about who we are and where we come from.

Taste

Light	Spirit Forward

Dry	Sweet

Skill

Easy	Advanced

Minutes	Hours

Ingredients

1 ½ oz	Ten To One Dark Rum
½ oz	Pineapple Rum
½ oz	Allspice Dram
½ oz	Pineapple Juice
½ oz	Averna Amaro
¼ oz	Tempus Fugit Creme de Banane
gn	Grated Nutmeg
	Dehydrated Pineapple

Glassware

Rocks

Instructions

01. Add all ingredients to a shaker tin with ice and shake vigorously for 15 to 20 seconds.
02. Strain into your glass over ice.
03. Garnish and serve.

High Tide

by Chauncey Smith

Inspiration

The Hide Tide is my twist on the legendary Mint Julep recipe mastered by one of the most renowned bartenders of all time, Tom Bullock. Tom's Juleps were so highly regarded that former President Roosevelt was widely known to have lied in a libel suit regarding his drinking habits after asserting he "only had a few sips of a Mint Julep" made by Bullock. As stated in The St. Louis Post-Dispatch "who was ever known to drink just a part of Tom's?"

Mr Bullock would go on to become the first African-American author to publish a cocktail manual with the release of The Ideal Bartender. I'm honored to be able to build on the foundation laid by Tom and the many other pioneers who have come before, many of whom had no idea of the legacy they would leave.

Taste

Light	Spirit Forward
Dry	Sweet

Skill

Easy	Advanced
Minutes	Hours

Ingredients

2 oz	Ten To One Dark Rum
½ oz	Butterfly Pea Flower Syrup*
1 oz	Lemon Juice
1 tsp	Ginger Preserve
5-6	Mint Leaves
	Soda Water
gn	Mint Sticks
	Lemon Wheel

Glassware

Collins

Instructions

01. In a shaker tin gently muddle the mint leaves and lemon juice.
02. Add remaining ingredients (excl. syrup & soda water) to shaker tin with ice and shake vigorously for 10 seconds.
03. Add syrup to the bottom of your glass and fill halfway with crushed ice.
04. Add mint leaves and more crushed ice to your glass.
05. Strain mixture gently into your glass and top with soda water.
06. Garnish and serve.

Specialty Ingredients

Syrups

Infusions & Washes

Special Recipes

Specialty Ingredients:
Syrups

Basil Mango Bulgogi Syrup

Ingredients

½ cup	Cane Sugar
½ cup	Water
¾ cup	Mango; diced
½ tsp	Bulgogi Marinade
3	Basil Leaves

Equipment

Saucepan   Fine Strainer
Measuring Cup
Glass Container

Instructions

01. Combine *water, mango, sugar, bulgogi marinade,* and *basil* in a small saucepan over medium-low heat until dissolved.
02. Bring to a light boil for 3 minutes.
03. Reduce to a medium/low heat and simmer for 10 minutes.
04. Remove from heat and let cool to room temperature.
05. Fine strain into an air tight glass container. Syrup will keep, refrigerated, for about one month.

Butterfly Pea Flower Syrup

Ingredients

1 cup	Granulated Sugar
½ cup	Water
10-15	Dried Butterfly Pea Flowers

Equipment

Saucepan   Fine Strainer
Glass Container
Measuring Cup

Instructions

01. Combine *water, sugar,* and *butterfly pea flowers* in a small saucepan over medium-low heat until dissolved.
02. Bring to a light boil and remove from heat.
03. Let cool to room temperature.
04. Fine strain into an air tight glass container. Syrup will keep, refrigerated, for about one month.

Black Cardamom Syrup

Ingredients

⅓ cup	Grade A Maple Syrup
⅛ cup	Black Cardamom Seeds
2 tsp	Water

Equipment

Saucepan   Strainer
Glass Container
Measuring Cup

Instructions

01. Combine *water, maple syrup,* and *cardamom seeds* in a saucepan over medium heat, stirring vigorously until sugar is completely dissolved.
02. Bring to a light boil for 30 seconds.
03. Remove from heat and let cool to room temperature.
04. Fine strain into an air tight glass container. Syrup will keep, refrigerated, for about one month.

Cane Sugar Syrup

Ingredients

½ cup	Cane Sugar
½ cup	Water

Equipment

Saucepan
Glass Container
Measuring Cup

Instructions

01. Combine *water* and *sugar* in a small saucepan over medium-low heat until dissolved.
02. Bring to a light boil and remove from heat.
03. Let cool to room temperature.
04. Store using a air tight glass container. Simple syrup will keep, refrigerated, for about one month.

Cardamom Blood Orange Syrup

Ingredients

1 cup	Light Brown Sugar
1 cup	Water
½ tsp	Ground Cardamom
3	Blood Orange; slices

Equipment

Saucepan
Measuring Cup
Glass Container
Fine Strainer

Instructions

01. Mix *cardamom* with *sugar* until well incorporated.
02. Combine *water,* and *sugar mixture* in a small saucepan over medium-low heat until dissolved.
03. Squeeze *blood orange slices* into saucepan before adding.
04. Simmer for 10 minutes and avoid bringing to a boil.
05. Remove from heat and let cool to room temperature.
06. Strain syrup through a mesh strainer into an air tight glass container. Syrup will keep, refrigerated, for about one month.

Chinese 5 Spice Syrup

Ingredients

2 cup	Distilled Water
2 cup	Granulated Sugar
½ tsp	Cloves
½ tsp	Red Pepper Flakes
¼ tsp	Ground Cinnamon
½ tsp	Fennel Seeds
2	Whole Star Anise

Equipment

Saucepan
Glass Container
Measuring Cup
Fine Strainer

Instructions

01. Heat the *water, cloves, red pepper flakes, cinnamon, fennel, star anise,* and *sugar* in a small saucepan over medium-low heat until dissolved.
02. Remove from heat and let cool to room temperature.
03. Fine strain into an air tight glass container. Syrup will keep refrigerated for about one month.

Cinnamon Syrup

Ingredients

1 cup	Granulated Sugar
1 cup	Water
2	Cinnamon Sticks

Equipment

Saucepan
Glass Container
Measuring Cup
Strainer

Instructions

01. Heat the *water, sugar,* and *cinnamon sticks* in a small saucepan over medium-low heat until dissolved.
02. Reduce heat to medium and let simmer for 10 minutes.
03. Remove from heat and let cool to room temperature.
04. Fine strain into an air tight glass container. Syrup will keep, refrigerated, for about one month.

Curried Simple Syrup

Ingredients

1 cup	Granulated Sugar
1 cup	Water
¼ cup	Jamaican Curry Powder

Equipment

Saucepan
Glass Container
Measuring Cup
Strainer

Instructions

01. Heat the *water, sugar,* and *Jamaican curry powder* in a small saucepan over medium-low heat until dissolved.
02. Let cool to room temperature.
03. Fine strain into an air tight glass container. Syrup will keep, refrigerated, for about one month.

Demerara Syrup

Ingredients

| 1 cup | Granulated Sugar |
| ½ cup | Water |

Equipment

Saucepan
Glass Container
Measuring Cup

Instructions

01. Combine the *water* and *sugar* in a small saucepan over medium-low heat until dissolved.
02. Bring to a light boil and remove from heat.
03. Let cool to room temperature.
04. Store using a air tight glass container. Simple syrup will keep, refrigerated, for about one month.

Honey Syrup

Ingredients

| ½ cup | Honey |
| ½ cup | Water |

Equipment

Saucepan   Fine Strainer
Glass Container
Measuring Cup

Instructions

01. Combine *water* and *honey* in a saucepan over medium heat, stirring vigorously until *honey* is completely dissolved.
02. Remove from heat and let cool to room temperature.
03. Store in an air tight glass container. Syrup will keep, refrigerated, for about one month.

Honey Ginger Syrup

Ingredients

1 cup	Honey
1 cup	Water
1	6" Piece of Ginger; sliced thin

Equipment

Saucepan   Cheesecloth
Glass Container
Measuring Cup

Instructions

01. Combine *water, honey* and *thinly sliced ginger* in a small saucepan over medium-low heat until dissolved.
02. Bring to a light boil. Reduce heat to medium and simmer for 5 minutes.
03. Remove from heat and let cool to room temperature before placing in the refrigerator to steep overnight.
04. Strain syrup through a cheesecloth into an air tight glass container. Syrup will keep, refrigerated, for about one month.

Orgeat

Ingredients

1 ½ cup	Granulated Sugar
1 ¼ cup	Water
2 cup	Blanched Almonds; ground
½ tsp	Orange Flower Water
1 oz	Ten To One White Rum

Equipment

Saucepan
Glass Container
Measuring Cup

Instructions

01. Combine *water* and *sugar* in a small saucepan over medium-low heat until dissolved. Bring to a light boil and add *Almonds*.
02. Reduce heat to medium and simmer for 3 minutes.
03. Remove from heat and let cool to room temperature before adding *orange*
04. *flower water.* Place in the refrigerator to steep for 3-8 hours.
    Strain syrup through a cheesecloth into an air tight glass container. Syrup will keep, refrigerated, for about one month.

Pineapple Syrup

Ingredients

½ cup   Pineapple Juice
½ cup   Cane Sugar
½ cup   Water

Equipment

Saucepan   Strainer
Glass Container
Measuring Cup

Instructions

01.   Combine *water, sugar,* and *pineapple* in a small saucepan over
      medium-low heat until dissolved. Bring to a light boil for 3 minutes.
02.   Reduce to a medium/low heat and simmer for 10 minutes.
03.   Remove from heat and Let cool to room temperature.
04.   Strain syrup through a mesh strainer into an air tight glass container.
      Syrup will keep, refrigerated, for about one month.

Pineapple Ginger Syrup

Ingredients

½ cup   Pineapple Juice
½ cup   Granulated Sugar
¼ cup   Ginger Root; finely chopped
¾ cup   Water

Equipment

Saucepan
Measuring Cup
Glass Container
Fine Strainer

Instructions

01.   Combine *water, sugar, pineapple* and *ginger* in a small saucepan over
02.   medium-low heat until dissolved.
03.   Add Ginger and Pineapple Juice, bringing the syrup to a light boil.
04.   Reduce heat to medium and let simmer for 10 minutes.
05.   Remove from heat and let cool to room temperature.
06.   Fine strain into an air tight glass container. Syrup will keep, refrigerated,
      for about one month.

Pineapple Gum Syrup

Ingredients

1 cup	Pineapple Juice
¾ cup	Granulated Cane Sugar
1 tsp	Agar Agar Powder

Equipment

Saucepan
Glass Container
Measuring Cup

Instructions

01. Combine *pineapple juice* and *sugar* in a saucepan over high heat until dissolved. Reduce to a medium heat and let simmer.
02. Add *agar agar powder* and stir until dissolved. You can adjust the ratio to achieve your desired level of thickness, but be warned a little goes a long way.
03. Remove from heat and let cool to room temperature.
04. Store using a air tight glass container. Simple syrup will keep, refrigerated, for about one month.

Pineapple Turmeric Syrup

Ingredients

½ cup	Pineapple Juice
½ cup	Cane Sugar
½ tsp	Turmeric Powder
½ tsp	Cracked Black Pepper

Equipment

Saucepan
Measuring Cup
Glass Container
Fine Strainer

Instructions

01. Combine *pineapple juice, sugar, turmeric powder,* and *black pepper* in a saucepan over medium heat until dissolved.
02. Bring to a light boil for 1 minute and remove from heat.
03. Let cool to room temperature.
04. Fine strain into an air tight glass container. Syrup will keep, refrigerated, for about one month.

Plantain Watermelon Syrup

Ingredients

½ cup   Plantain; diced
½ cup   Watermelon; diced
2 cup   Granulated Sugar
1 cup   Watermelon Juice

Equipment

Saucepan
Measuring Cup
Glass Container
Fine Strainer

Instructions

01.   Combine *watermelon juice, sugar, diced watermelon,* and *diced plantain* in a saucepan over medium heat until dissolved.
02.   Bring to a light boil for 30 seconds.
03.   Remove from heat and let cool to room temperature.
04.   Fine strain into an air tight glass container. Syrup will keep, refrigerated, for about one month.

Rich Simple Syrup

Ingredients

1 cup   Granulated Sugar
½ cup   Water

Equipment

Saucepan
Glass Container
Measuring Cup

Instructions

01.   Combine *water* and *sugar* in a small saucepan over medium-low heat until dissolved.
02.   Bring to a light boil and remove from heat.
03.   Let cool to room temperature.
04.   Store using a air tight glass container. Simple syrup will keep, refrigerated, for about one month.

Simple Syrup

Ingredients

½ cup   Granulated Sugar
½ cup   Water

Equipment

Saucepan
Glass Container
Measuring Cup

Instructions

01. Combine *water* and *sugar* in a small saucepan over medium-low heat until dissolved.
02. Bring to a light boil and remove from heat.
03. Let cool to room temperature.
04. Store using a air tight glass container. Simple syrup will keep, refrigerated, for about one month.

Sorrel Syrup

Ingredients

2 cup   Granulated Sugar
2 cup   Water
1 ½ cup   Dry Hibiscus Flower
5 oz   Rose Water
2 oz   Beet Juice

Equipment

Saucepan
Measuring Cup
Glass Container
Fine Strainer

Instructions

01. Heat the water in a small saucepan until boiling.
02. Add *hibiscus flower* and steep until the water turns amber.
03. Reduce to a medium heat and let simmer.
04. Add *sugar* and *beet juice* until dissolved
05. Remove from heat and let cool to room temperature.
06. Add *rose water*.
07. Fine strain into an air tight glass container. Syrup will keep, refrigerated, for about one month.

Wild Strawberry Syrup

Ingredients

1 lbs	Halved Strawberries
1 cup	Cane Sugar
2 cup	Water

Equipment

Saucepan   Strainer
Glass Container
Measuring Cup

Instructions

01.   In a small saucepan over high heat bring *water* and *strawberries* to a boil.

02.   Reduce heat to medium and let *strawberries* simmer for 15 minutes. Skim any excess foam that accumulates throughout.

03.   Reduce to a medium/low heat and remove *strawberries*.

04.   Add *sugar*, stirring on medium-low heat until dissolved.

05.   Remove from heat and let cool to room temperature.

06.   Strain syrup through a mesh strainer into an air tight glass container. Syrup will keep, refrigerated, for about one month.

Specialty Ingredients:
Infusions & Washes

Bacon Fat Washed Ten To One

Ingredients

13 oz   Ten To One Dark Rum
½ lb   Bacon

Equipment

Frying Pan
Non Reactive Container
Glass Container

Instructions

01.   Fry *bacon* in a large pan, being sure to save the grease.
02.   Add grease to a non reactive container with *Ten To One Dark Rum*.
03.   Cover container and freeze for 24 - 36 hours.
04.   Remove container from freezer and discard the frozen fat that has accumulated on top of the liquor.
05.   Fine strain into an air tight glass container. Fat washed rum will keep refrigerated for about two weeks.

Coffee-Infused Punt e Mes

Ingredients

25 oz   Punt e Mes
10 g   African Coffee Beans

Equipment

Saucepan
Measuring Cup
Glass Container

Instructions

01.   Combine *Punt e Mes* and *Coffee Beans* in a large non reactive container.
02.   Cover container and steep for 6 hours.
03.   Strain through a coffee filter into an air tight glass container. Infused Punt e Mes will keep, refrigerated, for about one month.

Green Tea Infused Ten To One

Ingredients

6 oz	Ten To One Dark Rum
1	Green Tea Bag

Equipment

Measuring Cup
Non Reactive Container
Glass Container

Instructions

01. Steep *green tea bag* in *Ten To One Dark Rum* using a non reactive container at room temperature for 4 minutes.
02. Remove *tea bag*. Do not squeeze.
03. Store in an air tight glass container. Infused rum will keep refrigerated for about a month.

Plantain & Ginger Infused Ten To One

Ingredients

25 oz	Ten To One Dark Rum
1	Plantain; diced
1	Ginger Root; diced

Equipment

Mason Jar
Fine Strainer
Glass Container

Instructions

01. Add *plantain* and *ginger* to mason jar and fill with *Ten To One Dark Rum*.
02. Cover jar with saran wrap before sealing with lid.
03. Let sit for 2 to 3 days agitating (shaking jar) twice daily.
04. Fine strain into an air tight glass container. Infused rum will keep, refrigerated, for about one month.

Specialty Ingredients:
Special Recipes

Acidulated OJ

Ingredients

| 99% | Orange Juice; fresh squeezed |
| 1% | Citric Acid |

Equipment

Glass Container

Instructions

01. Add 1% *citric acid* to total weight of *fresh squeezed juice* in a container and stir gently to combine.
02. Store in an air tight glass container. Juice will keep refrigerated for 2-3 days.

Chartreuse Foam

Ingredients

2 oz	Green Chartreuse
8 oz	Egg White
½ oz	Lemon Juice

Equipment

Whisk
Mixing Bowl
Soda Siphon

Instructions

01. Whisk all ingredients gently until incorporated.
02. Add to a soda siphon with an N^{02} charge.

Ethiopian Coffee

Ingredients

20 g	Ethiopian Coffee Beans
300 g	Hot Water

Equipment

Coffee Grinder
Coffee Filter
Glass Container

Instructions

01. Grind *coffee beans* for a pour over consistency (like coarse sea salt).
02. Add *coffee* to your coffee filter and pour hot water over grinds, allowing *coffee* to brew.
03. Let cool to room temperature.
04. Store in an airtight glass container. Coffee will keep refrigerated for 1-2 days.

Hibiscus Salt

Ingredients

½ tbsp	Pink Peppercorn
1 tbsp	Hibiscus Flower
½ tbsp	Tajin
½ tbsp	Brown Sugar

Equipment

Small Mixing Bowl
Plate

Instructions

01. Add all ingredients to a small mixing bowl and combine.
02. Pour mixture onto your plate ready to garnish.

Passion Fruit Purée

Ingredients

5 ea	Passion Fruit
5 tsp	Water

Equipment

Blender
Glass Container
Measuring Cup

Instructions

01. Cut the *passion fruit* in half cross-wise and scoop the seeds and pulp into a blender with *water*. Blend on high for two to three seconds.
02. Strain blended *passion fruit* through a mesh strainer. Use a wooden spoon
03. to help push the pulp through the strainer.
04. Store in an airtight glass container. Purée will keep, refrigerated, for about one week.

Spiced Pomegranate Cordial

Ingredients

16 oz	Rich Simple Syrup*
2 oz	Everclear
¼ oz	Rose Water
1 cup	Pomegranate Seeds
8 ds	Hellfire Bitters

Equipment

Non Reactive Container
Glass Container

Instructions

01. Heat *rich simple syrup* in a saucepan over medium heat until simmering.
02. Add *Hellfire Bitters* and *pomegranate seeds*, stirring until thickened.
03. Remove from heat and strain through a fine strainer.
04. Let cool to room temperature.
05. Add *Everclear* and *rose water*.
06. Store in an air tight glass container. Cordial will keep refrigerated for about a month.

Proudly presented by